T0114740

PERSEVERANCE DESPITE PUNISHMENT

(Get Out Of The Box)

DOROTHY LOTT

authorHOUSE®

AuthorHouse™
1663 Liberty Drive
Bloomington, IN 47403
www.authorhouse.com
Phone: 833-262-8899

Published by AuthorHouse 10/23/2023

ISBN: 979-8-8230-1472-4 (sc)
ISBN: 979-8-8230-1471-7 (e)

Library of Congress Control Number: 2023917761

Print information available on the last page.

This book is printed on acid-free paper.

Dedicated To The Memory Of My Late Mother

Ms. Elnora McDade

SOURCES OF BACKGROUND INFORMATION FOR SUBJECTS DISCUSSED:

*The King James Bible
*The Public Library
*A Gift of Heritage... Historic Black Women, Empak, Black History, "Publication Series."
*Extraordinary Black Americans, From Colonial to Contemporary Times. Susan Altman.
* All Poetry Is Exclusively That Of The Poet.

TABLE OF CONTENTS

WHY I WROTE THIS BOOK

We all start out as humans... newborn babies. We are created in the image of God.

We are sometimes labeled, and put in container boxes by people who know nothing of our gifts, talents, abilities, our genius, the Holy Spirit has placed within us.

Some accept the labels and reports others shave of them. "He or she will never amount to anything. They will have a house full of children and never marry. They will never finish high school or have a job."

Don't believe the reports. Refuse to accept the labels. Don't live your entire life on the expectations other have designed for your life.

You must step outside the containment of the simple minds of others. God has designed great things for your life outside the mind boxes of others. Believe it and receive it.

In this book, you will read the lives of people who refused to accept reports others had of them. They broke free from restraints, bondage and received their victories God had destined for them.

They persevered through many hardships. They did what they wanted to do. Through hard work and tenancy, they succeed and so can we.

COUSIN CUSH

She was tall,
When I was small.
She was old...
I was told.
Walked everywhere she went –
Without stoop or bent.
A woman can't be defined
Simply by her female parts.
Underneath her brimming lips
And swinging hips,
There stands her heart.
Men thought her a tough woman.
She was just one hot number.
She never walked on Mars.
She never bought cars.
Earth was her formation.
Her feet were her transportation.
I did see her house.
She probably never owned a
Respectable couch.
Tree stumps, at times, were her bed.
A resting place for her head.
She was just...
Just a part of planet earth...
The place of her splendid birth.

A place she recognized.
A place she didn't criticize.
Each stayed in harmony with the other.
Each heeded another.
Adam would have been proud
To call her wo-man.
She went by God's earth...
To pick some fruit.
It was bidden fruit...
Never forbidden fruit.
Her feet were as flat as the earth--
Probably born that way.
God's great Earth ——
Was made for her birth.
The soil was warm and sweet...
Underneath her flat feet.
That was very neat.

This land... where Jesus Stood.
This land... where I could.
This land... where we glean.
This land... where people dream.
This land... where cattle roam
This land... where we call home.
This land... where we stand by.
This land... where we come to die.
This land... where we feel and feed
This land... where we truly have need.
This land... where bees make honey.
This land... where we make our money.

This land... where Cain killed Abel

This land... where we meet our neighbors.

This land... where cars are made.

This land... where trees provide shade.

This land... where wars are fought.

This land... where we pay the cost.

This land... where humans love and mate.

This land... where we scheme and hate.

This land... where we consume water and food.

This land... where mountains stand nude.

This land... where we sit.

This land... where we cuss and spit.

This land... where God destroyed Sodom and Gomorrah.

This land... where God saved Noah.

This land... where we claim the known.

This land... where God truly owns.

This land... where Moses parted the Red Sea.

This land... where the Israelites went free.

This land... where David stood.

This land... where Goliath fell.

This land... where he delights

This land... where we pursue our education.

This land... where we feed our imagination.

This land... where medicine comes from.

This land... where Gods saves and heals.

This land... where people seal their deals.

This land... where yesterday has gone.

This land... where today is not known.

This land... where tomorrow is unknown.

This land... where mile links to mile.

This land... where we look up and smile.

This land... where beauty takes our breath.
This land... where we lie down and rest.
This land... where we stand bold.
This land... where Bibles are sold.
This land... where God knows how old.
This land... where man stores his treasure.
This land... where we seek our pleasure

This land... where we connive.
This land... where we strive.
This land... where we grow old.
This land... where God lightens our load.
This land... where all humans are created in the image of God.
This land... where we all have different skin colors.
This land... where we disrespect each other.
This land... where we connect with each other
This land... where we disconnect with each other.
This land... where we show discontent toward others.
This land... where God gives us agape Love.
This land... where it can only come from above.
This land... where the adversary dwells.
This land... where God created hell.
This land... where we consume our doubts.
This land... where God is all about.
This land... where we repent.
This land... where grace is scent.
This land... where our ancestors rest.
This land... where they gave their best.
This land... is not our land.
This land... will go back to the earth.
This land... where God gave its' birth.

GET OUT OF THAT BOX

Boxes were made for gifts...
humans were never made to fit.
Finding yourself in one...
is never any fun.
You don't have to stay...
you can crash out any day.
No matter what others say...
just jump out and breathe,
and get what God wants you to receive.
Simply, break free.
There's a whole new world to see.

Freedom awaits the daring...
the humble and the caring.
There's so much to receive,
because we have great needs.

You may have been told,
you can never escape the box.
But you must be bold.
Outside the box, freedom is permitted.
Outside the box, people cannot be contained.
Outside the box, your gifts are nourished.
Outside the box, you can flourish.
The box annihilates.
So, don't stay in and suffocate.

THOSE WHO STEPPED
OUTSIDE THE BOX

Naomi's box was Moab...
Dead, dull and drab.
She suffered loss in her box...
Doom and gloom.
She was left utterly stunned,
After the loss of her 2 sons.
The Moab box put a damper
On her hopes and dreams.

Naomi decided one day to break out...
To defy her fears and doubts.
Naomi's daughter-in-law Ruth went to.
She did what she had to do.
Naomi mentored Ruth.
This was her greatest pursuit.

Ruth was a woman led by faith.
She refused to stay one more day.
She stepped into the life of Boaz...
In her box she never could have.
Her name landed in the Holy Bible.
Her descendant's genealogy consists of **King David,
King Solomon,** and our savior, **Jesus Christ**.

Ruth 1:1, 2, 3, 5, 22

Now it came to pass in the days when the judges ruled, that there was a famine in the land. And a certain man of Beth-lehem-Judah went to sojourn in the country of Moab, he, and his wife, and his two sons. And the name of the man was Elimelech. And the name of his wife Naomi, and the name of his two sons Mahlon and Chilion. Ephrathites of Beth-lehem-Hudah. And they came into the country of Moab, and continued there.

And Elimelech Naomi's husband died; and she was left, and her two sons.

And Mahlon and Chilion died also both of them: And the woman was left of her two sons and her husband. So Naomi returned, and Ruth the Moabitess, her daughter-in-law, with her, which returned out of the country of Moab: and they came to Bethlehem in the beginning of Barley Harvest.

<u>Ruth</u> 2:3

And she went, and came, and gleaned in the field after the reapers: and her hap was to light on a part of the field belonging unto Boaz, who was of the kindred of Elimelech.

<u>Ruth</u> 4:13, 17

So Boaz took Ruth, and she was his wife: and when he went in unto her, the Lord gave her conception, and she bare a son.

And the women her neighbors gave it a name saying. There is a son born to Naomi: and they called his name Obed: he is the father of Jesse, the father of David.

ABRAHAM

God ordered Abram to leave his hometown in Haran.
For Abram, this could have been very daring.
With God's orders He is very caring.
Abram knew not where he was going.
He was to lead a life of sacrifice and sowing.
The king of Salem blessed Abram with the tithe.
This of him was extremely wise.
God tested Abram by ordering him to sacrifice his son.
This for Abram was no fun.
Through Abram's obedience God saved Abram's son.
God unboxed Abram and he became known as **Abraham.**
Abraham *Believed God.*
Abraham *trusted God.*
Abraham *obeyed God.*
Abraham *was a friend of God.*
God accounted Abraham's faith and obedience for righteousness.
God promised Abraham that he would make him the
the father of many nations.
God said that Abraham's ancestor would be as numerous as the
stars in the sky and the sand by the seashore.

Genesis 12:1, 2, 4

Now the Lord had said unto Abram, get thee out of thy country, and from thy kindred, and from thy father's house, unto a land that I will show thee:

And I will make thee a great nation, and I will bless Thee, make thy name great: and thou shalt be a blessing:

So Abram departed, as the Lord had spoken unto him: and Lot went with him: and Abram was seventy and five years old when he departed out of Haran.

Genesis 14:18, 19, 20

And Melchizedek king of Salem brought forth bread and wine: and he was the priest of the most high God.

And he blessed him, and said Blessed be Abram of the most high God, possessor of heaven and earth:

And blessed be the most high God, which hath delivered thine enemies into thy hand. And he gave him tithes of all.

Genesis 17:5

Neither shall thy name any more be called Abram, but thy name shall be Abraham: for a father of many nations have I made the

Genesis 22:1, 2, 10, 11, 12

And it came to pass after these things, that God did tempt Abraham, and said unto him, Abraham: and he said, Behold, here I am.

And he said, take now thy son, thine only son Isaac, whom Thou lovest and get thee into the land of Moriah: and offer him there for a burnt offering unto one of the mountains Which I will tell thee of.

And Abraham stretched forth his hand, and took the the knife to slay his son. And the Angel of the Lord called unto him out of heaven, and said, Abraham, Abraham: and he said, here am I.

And he said, lay not thine hand upon the lad, neither do thou any thing unto him: for now, I know that thou fearest God, seeing thou hast not withheld thy son, thine only son.

MOSES

God gave Moses a commission.
Moses was not willing for the position.

God had heard the Israelites cry.
He could no longer stand silently by.
They had suffered many hundreds of years as slaves. They had dug
many thousands of graves.

After much dialogue with God... Moses finally did consent, and
away to Egypt and Pharaoh he went.

Moses delivered the Israelites from being slaves, otherwise, they
probably would have stayed –– in discomfort and shame. There
was no hope of any gain.

They left Egypt happy and bold.
Their donkeys were loaded down with fine gold.
They were all healthy and well.
As the scriptures so eloquently tell.

Moses brought God's people out of their box...of poverty, pain,
shame and disdain.
God never promised us pain.
He wants us to obtain beauty and pleasure...
beyond what our feeble human imagination can ascertain.

<u>EXODUS</u> 3:1, 2, 4, 5, 6, 10, 11

Moses kept the flock of Jethro his father-in-law, the priest of Midian: and he led the flock to the backside of the desert, and came to the mountain of God, Horeb. And the angel of the Lord appeared unto him in a flame of fire out of the midst of a bush: and he looked, and behold, the bush burned with fire, and the bush was not consumed.

And when the Lord saw that he turned aside to see, God called unto him out of the midst of the bush, and said, Moses, Moses. And he said, Here am I. And he said, draw not nigh hither: put off they shoes off thy feet, for the place whereon thou standest is holy ground.

More ever he said, I am the God of thy father, the God of Abraham, the God of Isaac, and the God of Jacob. And Moses hid his face: for he was afraid to look upon God. And the Lord said, I have surely seen the affliction of my people which are in Egypt, and have heard their cry by reason of their taskmasters: for I know their sorrows: come now therefore, and I will send thee unto Pharaoh, that thou mayest bring forth my people the children of Israel out of Egypt. And Moses said unto God, who am I, that I should go unto Pharaoh, and that I should bring forth the children of Israel out of Egypt?

Exodus 3:21, 22   *Exodus* 4:18, 20

And Moses went and returned to Jethro his father in law, and said unto him, let me go, I pray thee, and return unto my brethren which are in Egypt, and see whether they be yet alive. And Jethro said to Moses, go in peace.

And Moses took his wife and his sons, and set them Upon an ass, and he returned to the land of Egypt: and Moses took the rod of God in his hand.

And I will give their people favor in the sight of the Egyptians: and it shall come to pass, that, when ye go, ye shall not go empty:

But every woman shall borrow of her neighbor, and of her that sojourneth in her house, jewels of silver and *jewels of gold, and rainment: and ye shall put them upon your sons and upon your daughters: and ye shall spoil the Egyptians.*

EXODUS *12:38, 41*

And a mixed multitude went up also with them; and flock, and herds, even very mush cattle.

And it came to pass at the end of the four hundred and thirty years, even the selfsame day it came to pass, that all of the host of the Lord went out from the land of Egypt.

JOSHUA AND CALEB

Moses sent 12 men to spy out the land of Canaan,
10 came back with a bad report.
They saw the giants.
Their faith was smaller than the giants
Joshua and Caleb stilled the people before Moses.
Their faith was greater than the giants.
They said, "Lets' go up at once and possess it; for we are well able
to take it."
In Canaan, the grapes were _Grapelicious_.
The pomegranates were _Perlicious_.
The figs were _Figlicious_.
Joshua and Caleb perceived a new nation.
They were ready to break out of the wilderness box.
Eventually, their faith led them all the way to the _Promise Land._
The 10 spies along with their incredulity and trepidation, died in
the wilderness.
Fear can sometimes be a deadly persuasion.

NUMBERS 13:1, 2, 3, 17, 18, 23, 25, 26, 27, 28, 30, 31, 33, 38

And the Lord spake unto Moses, saying Send thou men, that they may search the land of Canaan, which I give unto the children of Israel: of every tribe of their fathers shall ye send a man, everyone a ruler among them.

And Moses by the commandment of the Lord sent them from The wilderness of Paran: all those men were heads of the children of Israel.

And Moses sent them to spy out the land of Canaan, and said unto them, get you up this way southward, and go up into the mountains:

And see the land, what it is, and the people that dwelleth therein, whether they be strong or weak, few or many.

So, they went up, and searched the land from the wilderness of Zin unto Rehob, as men come Hamath.

And they came unto the brook of Eshcol, and cut down from Thence a branch with one cluster of grapes, and they bare it between two upon a staff; and they brought of the Pomegranates, and of the figs. And they returned from searching of the land after forty days. And they went and came to Moses, and Aaron, and to all the congregation of the children of Israel, unto the wilderness of Paren, to Kadesh; and brought back word unto them, and unto all the congregation, and shewed them the fruit of the land. And they told him, and said we came unto the land whither thou sentest us, and surely it floweth with milk and honey; and this is the fruit of it. Nevertheless the people be strong that dwell in the land, and the cities are walled, and very great: and more over we saw the children of Anak there.

And Caleb stilled the people before Moses, and said, let us go up at once, and possess it, for we are well able to overcome it. But the men that went up with him said, we be not able to go up against the people; for they are stronger than we. And there we saw the giants: the sons of Anak, which come of the giants: and we were in our own sight as grasshoppers, and so we were in their sight.

But Joshua the son of Nun, and Caleb the son of Jephunneb, which were of the men that went to search the land, lived still.

THE HEBREW BOYS

The Hebrew Boys... by request from a crazy king...
was ordered to bow or burn.
The boys refused to bow to a king.
God was their only king.
The furnace was heated 7 times hotter,
the boys were thrown into a fiery furnace.
As the furnace burned...
the boys stood firm.
They knew their fate,
dictated a new day.
Because the boys refused to bow to a crazy king...
they were not burned.
When God stepped in...
they were bound to win.
The boys stepped out...
without a hint of doubt.
The crazy king did repent.
He could not defy the evidence.
Shadrach, Meshach and Abedego were promoted
In the providence.

Daniel *3:14, 15, 17, 18, 19, 20, 22,*
24, 25, 26, 27, 28, 29, 30

Nebuchadnezzar spake and said
unto them, Is it true, O Shadrach,
Meshach, and Abednego do not serve
my, gods nor worship the golden
image which I have set up? Now if ye
be ready that at which time ye hear
the sound of the cornet, flute, harp,
sachbut, psaltery, and dulcimer, and
all kinds of music, ye fall down and
worship the image which I have made:
well but if ye worship not, ye shall be
cast the same hour into the midst of
a burning fiery furnace: and who is
that God that shall deliver you out of
my hands?
If it be so, our God whom we serve is
able to deliver us from the burning

fiery furnace, and he will deliver us out of thine hands O king. But if not, be it known unto thee, O king, that we will not serve thy gods, nor worship the golden image which thou has set up. Then Nebuchadnezzar full of fury, and the form of his visage was changed against Shadrach, Meshach, and Abednego: therefore, he spake and commanded that they should heat the furnace seven seven times more than it was wont be heated.

And he commanded the most mighty men that were in his army to bind Shadrach, Meshach, and Abednego and cast them into the burning fiery furnace. And these three men Shadrach, Meshach, and Abednego, fell down bound into the midst of the Burning fiery furnace. Then Nebuchadnezzar the king was astonied, and, and rose up in haste, and spake, and said unto his counsellors, did not we cast three men bound into the midst of the fire? They answered and said unto the king, true, O king. He answered and said, lo, I see four men loose, walking in the midst of the fire, and they have no hurt: and the form of the fourth is like the Son of God.

Then Nebuchadnezzar came near to the mouth of the burning fiery furnace, and spake, and said, Shadrach, Meshach, and Abednego, ye servants of the most high God, come forth, and they came hither. Then Shadrach, Meshach, and Abednego, came forth, of the midst of the fire. And the Princess, governors, and captains, and the king's counsellors, being gathered together, saw these men, upon whose bodies the fire had no power, nor was a hair of their head singed, neither were their coats changed, nor the smell of fire passed on them.

Then Nebuchadnezzar spake, and said, blessed be the God of Shadrach, Meshach, and Abednego who hath sent his angel, and delivered his servants that trusted in him, and changed the king's word, and yielded their bodies, that they might not serve nor worship any god, except their own God

Therefore I make a decree that every people, nation, and language, which speak anything amiss against the God of Shadrach, Meshach, and Abednego, shall be made a dung hill, because there is no other God that can deliver after this sort.

Then the king promoted Shadrach, Meshach, and Abednego in the providence of Babylon.

THE WOMAN WHO TOUCHED JESUS

Twelve years of doctors she went.
Twelve years of money she spent.
The woman with the issue of blood...
Heard about Jesus one day.
She decided He was her only way.
She was dying in her box.
Her life was destined for pure rot.
To her... Jesus was grand.
She decided to take a stand.
The crowds were great,
But Jesus was her only fate.
In her box was death.
Jesus is life.
Her life contained confinement.
She made Jesus her assignment.
Tired and determined...
Bound and beguiled...
The crowds pushed her back.
But, she refused to give up the fight.
Low and bent... she slowly went.
At the him of His garment, she did relent.
She grabbed the mantle of life,
And forever rid herself of all strife.
This made for her a great life.

LUKE 8:43, 44, 45, 46, 47, 48

And a woman having an issue of blood twelve years, which had spent all her living upon physicians, neither could be healed of any, came behind him, and touched the border of his garment: and immediately her issue of blood stanched. And Jesus said, who touched me? when all denied, Peter And they that were with him said, master, the multitude throng thee and press thee, and sayest, thou, who touched me? and Jesus said, somebody hath touched me: for I perceive that virtue is gone out of me. And when the woman saw that she was not hid, she came trembling, and falling down before him, she declared unto him before all the people for what cause she had touched him, and how she was healed immediately. And he said unto her, Daughter, be of good comfort: thy faith hath made thee whole, go in peace.

ESTHER

Esther was a knockout
when she came out of her box.
Esther was a king's dream...
a lovely sight to be seen.
She found favor with a king.
Esther was chosen by a king,
to become his queen...
for all to be seen.
Esther's evil adversary was
a man name Hamon.
He wanted the Jewish people destroyed.
Esther was tested.
She defeated her adversary.
Esther saved the Jewish Nation.
A Bible Book bears her name.
She and her people would never be the same.

<u>*ESTHER*</u> *2:8-9 3:8, 9 4:4, 5, 6, 7, 8,*
9, 10 4:11, 12, 13, 14, 15, 16, 9:24,
25 9:26, 32 10:3

So it came to pass, when the king's
commandment And his decree was
heard, and when many maidens
were gathered together unto Shushan
the palace, to the custody of Hegai,
that Esther was brought also, unto
the king's house, to the custody of
Hegai, keeper of the women. And the
maiden pleased him, and she obtained
kindness of him: and he speedily gave
her things for purification, with such
things as belonged to her, and seven
maiden which were meet to be given
her, out of the king's house: and he
preferred her and her maids unto the
best places of the house of the women.

And Haman said unto king Ahasuerus, there is a certain people scattered abroad and dispersed among the people in all the provinces of the kingdom: and their laws are diverse from all people: neither keep they the king's laws: therefore, it is not for the king's profit to suffer them.

If it please the king, let it be written that they may be destroyed: and I will pay ten thousand talents of silver to the hands of those that have the charge of the business, to bring it unto the king's treasuries.

So, Esther's maids and her chamberlains came and told it to her. Then was the queen exceedingly grieved: and she sent rainment to clothe Mordecai, and to take away his sackcloth from him: but he received it not.

Then called Esther for Hatach, one of the king's chamberlains, whom he had appointed to attend upon her, and gave him a commandment to Mordecai, to know what it was, and why it was.

So Hatach went forth to Mordecai unto the street of the city, which was before the king's gate.

And Mordecai told him of all that had happened unto him, and of the sum of money that Haman had promised to pay to the king's treasuries for the Jews, to destroy them. Also, he gave him the copy of the writing of the decree that was given at Shushan to destroy them, to show it unto Esther, and to declare it unto her, and to charge her that she should go in unto the king, to make supplication unto him, and to make request before him for her people.

And Hatach came and told Esther the words of Mordecai. And Esther spake unto Hatach, to give him commandment unto Mordecai.

And the king's servants, and the people of the king's Provinces, do know, that whosoever, whether man or woman, shall come unto the king into the inner court, who is not called, there is one law of his to put him to death, except such to whom the king shall hold out the golden septre, that he may live: but I have not been called to come in unto the king these thirty days.

And they told to Mordecai Esther's words. Then Mordecai commanded to answer Esther, think not with thyself that thou shalt escape in the king's house more than all the Jews.

For if thou altogether holdest thy peace at this time, then shall their enlargement and deliverance arise to the Jews from another place, but thou and thy father's house shall be destroyed: and who knoweth whether thou are come to the kingdom for such a time as this?

Then Esther bade them return Mordecai this answer. Go gather together all the Jews that are present in Shushan and fast ye for me, and neither eat nor drink three days:

I also and my maidens will fast likewise: and so will I go in unto the king, which is not according to the law: and if I perish, I perish.

Because Haman the son of Hammedatha, the Agagite, the enemy of all the Jews, had devised against the Jews to destroy them, and had cast pier that, the lot, to consume them, and to destroy them.

But when Esther came before the king, he commanded by Letters that his wicked devise, whish he devised against the Jews, should return upon his own head, and that he and his sons should be hanged on the gallows, and the decree of Esther confirmed these matters of Purim, and it was written in the book.

For Mordecai the Jew was next unto king Asasuerus and great among the Jews, and accepted of the multitude of his brethren, seeking the wealth of his people, and speaking to all his seed.

PAUL

In his box, his name was Saul.
Outside of the box he became known as Paul.
Saul left his box on the Damascus trail.
The angels in Heaven let out a wail.
Paul stepped into his Godly Assignment...
from a life of sin and confinement.
His marvelous works had already been predestined...
as many lost souls awaited.
His box was defeated.
He fought a good fight.
He finished his course.
He kept the faith.
Paul now sits in Heavenly Places...
decorated with a crown filled with precious jewels,
too costly to be replaced.

ACTS 9:1, 2, 3, 4, 5, 6, 7, 8, 9, 10, 11, 17 19:11-12

And Saul yet breathing out threatenings and slaughter against the disciples of the Lord, went unto the high priest, and desired of him letters to Damascus to the synagogues, that if he found any of this way, whether they were men or women, he might bring them bound unto Jerusalem.

And as he journeyed, he came near Damascus: and suddenly there shined round about him a light from heaven: and he fell to the earth, and heard a voice saying unto him. Saul, Saul why persecutes thou me?

And he said, who art thou, Lord? And the Lord said, I Am Jesus whom thou persecutes: it is hard for thee to kick Against the pricks.

And the men which journed with him stood speechless, hearing a voice but seeing no man.

And Saul arose from the earth: and when his eyes were open, he saw no man: but they led him by hand, and brought him into Damascus.

And he was there three days without sight, and neither did eat nor drink

And there was a certain disciple at Damascus, named Ananias: and to him said the Lord in a vision, Ananias. And he said, behold, I am here, Lord.

And the Lord said unto him, arise, and go into the street which is called Straight, and inquire in the house of Judas for one called Saul of Tarsus: and enter in the house: and putting his hands on him said. Brother Saul, the Lord, even Jesus, that appeared unto thee in the way as thou camest, hath sent me, that thou mightiest receive thy sight, and be filled with the Holy Ghost.

And God wrought special miracle by the hands of Paul: So that from his body were brought unto the sick handkerchiefs or aprons, and the diseases departed from them, and the evil spirits went out of them.

I have fought a good fight, I have finished my course, I have kept the faith: Henceforth there is laid up for me a crown of righteousness, which the Lord, the righteous judge, shall give me at that day: and not to me only, but unto all them also that love his appearing. (2 Timothy 4:7, 8)

DAVID

OBED...THE SON OF RUTH
JESSE... THE SON OF OBED
SOLOMON... THE SON OF DAVID
RUTH... THE GREAT-GRAND-MOTHER OF DAVID

A shepherd boy was David
He tended his father, Jesse's sheep.
A lion and bear, one day... took a lamb...
From David's fold.
Without fear or hesitation...
David retrieved the little lamb.
David perceived this to be his destiny.
He smote both bear and lion.
He was tenacious.
He was robust.
He was courageous.
David was filled with faith.
As a continuous of his accolades...
David played a mean harp.
When Saul was full of evil spirits
David played his harp and the evil spirits departed.
His faith in God led him to kill the
Philistine giant, Goliath...
With a sling and one smooth stone.

1 Samuel 17:12, 22, 23, 32, 34, 35, 36, 40, 45, 46, 49, 51

Now David was the son of that Ephrathite of Beth-lehem-Judah, whose name was Jesse, and he had eight sons: and the Man went among men for an old man in the days of Saul And David left his carriage in the hands of the keeper of the carriage ran into the army and came and saluted his brethren. And as he talked with them, behold, there came up the champion, the Philistine of Gath, Goliath by name, out of the army of the Philistines, and spake according to the same words: and David heard them. And David said to Saul. Let no man's heart fail because of him, thy servant will go and fight with this

Philistine. And David said to Saul, thy servant kept his father's sheep, and there came a lion and a bear, and took a lamb out of the flock: And I went out after him, and smote him, and delivered it out of his mouth: and when he arouses against me, I caught him by his beard and smote him and slew him.

Thy servant slew both lion and bear: and this uncircumcised Philistine shall be as one of them, seeing he hath defiled the Armies of the living God.

And he took his staff in his hand, and chose him five smooth stones out of the brook, and put them in a shepherd's bag which he had, even in script; and he drew near to the Philistine. Then said David to the Philistine. Thou comest to me with sword, and with A spear, and with a shield; but I come to thee in the name of the Lord of host, the God of the armies of Israel, whom thou hast defied. This day will the Lord deliver thee into mine hand; and I will smite Thee and take thine head from thee; and I will give the carcasses of the host of the Philistines this day unto the fowls of the air, and to the wild beast of the earth; that all they may know that there is a God in Israel. And all the assembly know

*that the Lord saveth not with sword
And spear; for the battle is the Lord's
and he will give you into our hands.
And David put his hand in his bag,
and took thence a stone, and slang
it, and smooth the Philistine in his
forehead, that the stone sank into his
forehead; and he fell upon his face
to the earth. Therefore, David ran,
and stood upon the Philistine, and
took his sword, and drew it out of the
sheath thereof, and slew him, and cut
off his head therewith. And when the
Philistines saw their champion was
dead, they fled.*

HARRIETT TUBMAN

Harriett Tubman was nor cut out for slavery.
Subsequently, she decided to abandon the slave box.
There was no debate.
She knew she had to escape.
Freedom occupied her mind.
The only thing she had was time.
She was fearless and brave...
determined not to be nobody's slave.
She held her head high...
when danger came nigh.
Harriett was born in Maryland in 1859.
She left children and husband.
She rescued seventy enslaved families after 13
Missions. This was the Underground Railroad.
This was Miss Tubman's determined mission.
She returned to the South 19 times,
each time with freedom on her mind.
She became an American Abolitionist, Humanitarian,
an Army Scout, and a spy for the United States Army
during the Civil War.
This woman did all this through destiny and pure might
She was some kind of woman, alright.

MRS FANNIE LOU HAMER

1917-1977
Born in Ruleville, Mississippi
"Civil Rights Activist"

No matter the education...
No matter the poverty...
No matter the skin color...
No matter how deprived...
No matter where one lives...
No matter the name...
No matter the pain...
No matter the shame...

The will of a person to succeed can often out-weigh
their circumstances.
So it was...
with Mrs. Fannie Lou Hamer.

Her greatest pursuit-dream-desire was for the rights
of Black People to vote.
This was a fight she was willing to pursue.
It almost cost her, her life.

<u>Miss. Fannie Lou,</u>
born poor, October 6, 1917
in Ruleville, Mississippi,
youngest of 20 children.

Their survival was on a sharecropping plantation.
The entire family had to work together.
This deprived her of an education.
Food was scarce.

She married at age 24
and adapted 2 children.

Civil Rights Groups came to her community
In 1962. Mrs. Hamer involved herself with the
Civil Rights Movement.

She and others went to the courthouse to vote.
They were denied because of their skin color.
Racism was high in Mississippi.

A written test was designed by whites... for
Blacks People only.
The 21 questions consisted of
the state laws of Mississippi,
and the Constitution.
They all failed the test.

Mrs. Hamer promised she would be back
and would pass the test.
She did go back. She passed the test.

With a breathing body, hard work...
a strong will and great determination,
almost anything can be accomplished,
despite adversity.

Because of this woman's determination and
accomplishments...
she was made to pay a price.
Because of the color of her skin, she was beaten
within inches of her life.
She lost everything she owned...was thrown into jail.
Dr. Martin Luther King demanded her release.
She suffered great harassment... was followed
everywhere she went... attacked, spat on and shot at.
The racist made her life a living hell.

Her fierce determination outweighed her circumstances.
Mrs. Hamer was a force to reckoned with.

    *She was a strong, forceful speaker.
    After speaking at the National Democratic
    Convention: she received a standing ovation.
    Nothing could keep her down.
    To greater heights she did abound.

    *She raised over 1 million dollars for her
    District of Sunflower County.
    *She built a 680-acre farm to feed the needy
    of all races.
    *She started a day care center for women of
    working mothers.
    *She was the first black woman to run for congress
    In Mississippi.
    *She was the leader of the Loyalist Democratic Party.

*Mrs. Hamer stated, "I am tired of being sick and tired."

*She also stated in speaking of racism, "this ain't just Mississippi's problem. It's America's problem."

> John Wesley's Aphorism was
>   "Do all the good you can,
>   by all the means you can,
>   in in all the ways you can,
>   in all the times you can,
>   to all the people you can,
>   as long as you can."

I would gleefully say, "Mrs. Hamer gave out her life for the good of humanity."

Benjamin Bannaker, a black man, 1731-1806, Inventor, Surveyor, Mathematician and Astronomer stated, "The color of skin is in no way connected with strength of mind or intellectual powers."

Benjamin Bannaker constructed the first clock built in the United States. He dictated a Solar Eclipse, help... design the city of Washington DC., near Baltimore, Maryland. He built a pocked watch, made entirely of wood. It kept time for over forty years.

IDA B. WELLS BARNETT

1862––1931
BORN IN HOLY SPRINGS, MISSISSIPPI
JOURNALIST, ACTIVIST

Way down in Holly Springs, Mississippi
a child is born.
Ida B. Wells was her name.
A gift from Heaven.
Born to parents who were enslaved, keeping
in mind, slavery was man made.
God intended for humans to be free.
Slavery was never meant to be.

Slavery is an evil misery commiserated upon
certain humans by other humans.

Ida became parentless at age 14.
Her parents were gone, but she had to go on.
Her younger siblings became her responsibility.
There was no time for hostility.

Life was rough, but Ida was tough.
She possessed uncompromising determination.
She wanted to make for herself and others
a better life.
She persevered through horrendous strife.

Ida joined academia at Rust College down in
Mississippi... furthering her education at Fisk
University in Tennessee.

Ida became a teacher.
Achievements are sometimes gained
through much pain.

Miss Wells was brave.
She was a woman self-made.
She was unafraid to speak up.

She embarked on a lifelong anti-slavery crusade.
Becoming a writer Gave her a voice.
She knew she had a choice.
She wrote anti-slavery articles for the Free
Speech Newspaper; later becoming part owner
editor for the paper.

Her voice of prestige afforded her many
opportunities. She traveled, investigated, wrote
and told of lynching's throughout the South.
Her crusade took her all the way to England.

She lived during a time of
high lynching's, rampant racism, little love,
much hate and almost no opportunities for blacks.
These dire statistics were onerous, they
were blatant (vociferous).
Miss Wells was tenacious. Her spirit was vivacious.

She lost her teaching job in Memphis.
Her newspaper office was burned.
Yet she stood stern.

There was no time to look back.
She knew she had to fight.
Despite of opposition, she had a proposition.

What Rosa Parks did in 1955...
Ida Wells did the same thing about 100 years earlier.

Ida sat in an area on a bus designated for whites only.
After refusing to give up her seat; she was forcefully
removed from the bus. She went to court.
She sued and won her case.
She encouraged blacks not to ride the busses:
many did not. Some moved away.
The company almost went bankrupt.

After moving to New York.
She was yet persistent.
I guess you could say, she was insistent.
When people give you nothing.
You must insist upon something.
She was a force of resistance against the brutality
of lynching, combating the unfair treatment of her
people were her life's work.

She met and married Ferinand Barnett.
He was a lawyer and newspaper man.
They produced a family.
The fought the battle for a better life for
themselves and others.

   *Mrs. Barnett was co-founder of the (NAACP).
   *She fought for Women's Rights.
   *She marched with over 5.000 women
   in Washington D.C.
   She worked long, she worked hard.
   She became famous.
   *She received many honors.
   *A housing project in Chicago bears her name.

Miss Wells started out no-where, but she took her life somewhere.

Sometimes opportunities are given.
Sometimes opportunities are not given.
Sometimes they are taken away.
Sometimes we must make our own.
Sometimes we must seek, search and find.
Sometimes they are scarce.
Sometimes they are plentiful.

We should know and be grateful, that there were black people
like Ida B Wells Barnett... fighting before us... for us, all the time.

SOJOURNER TRUTH

1797-1882
ULSTER COUNTY, NEW YORK
AUTHOR, PREACHER, ACTIVIST, WOMEN'S RIGHT
ACTIVIST, ABOLITIONIST, HUMAN RIGHT'S ACTIVIST,
CIVIL RIGHT'S ACTIVIST.

Born Isabella Bumfree...
she was anything but free.
Being sold into slavery four times...
laid heavy upon her mind.

She bore many children...
most were sold into slavery.
A five-year-old son was sold and sent to Alabama.
Quakers helped her win him back.
That was a tough fight.

She often cried out in grief.
Only God heard her plea.
For Sojourner life was a rough ride
It only made sense with God on her side.

After God gave her a new name,
her life was destined for change.
Sojourner's quest for herself and others
was to be free.
This was her loudest plea,

Her mother taught her to pray.
Sometimes not knowing the right words to say...
but her faith stood strong.
She knew she was never alone.

She said God told her to travel,
and proclaim his name.
she walked hundreds of miles...
not knowing where she would sleep or eat.
She preached, prayed, taught and sang.
God did provide.

Her best speech, "Ain't I a woman," became widely
known during the Civil War. She spoke Dutch.

*First black woman to win a case in court
against a white man.
*Truth was inducted into the Women's Hall
Of Fame in 1981 in Seneca Fall, New York.
*Included in the Smithsonian Magazine list of
100 most significant women of all times.
*Her bust was unveiled in 2009 in Emancipation
Hall in the U.S. Capital Visitor's Center.
*In 1986 the U.S. Postal Service issued a
Commerative 22 cent Postage Stamp of her.

*A church in Ohio unveiled a Historical Marker
where she gave her famous speech.

*She was the first black person to have
a statue in the Capital Building.

*She is credited with the song "Valiant Solders."

*She spoke at the National Women's Rights
Convention in 1854.

*She purchased a home for 300 dollars.

*She met important people like William Lloyd
Garrison, Frederick Douglass, the president,
Abraham Lincoln. Susan B. Anthony was her
Friend.
*She helped recruit black troops during the
Civil War.

* Sojourner Truth Library at Paltz, State University
was named in honor in 1971 in New York.

When you dream and get up and make it come true there's
no limit what God can and will do.

HANGING OUT

Breezy and freezing
makes for a crisp November –
even crisper December.
Declining soft sweet mornings leave the sky jaded.
Sunrays sprinkle themselves yellow
and blemish over the
tear-stained waters of the Atlantic Ocean.

The dimly polishing sun striking
all that's left over from seasons long-ago –
rested their cases.
A faded bare leaf – a jagged hair threaded blade grass –
a blossomless bush – a tree,
awaiting Spring's permission.

A Phainopepla Bird paints the purpose of flight.
A chicken knows nothing about cooking oil,
but lays anyway.

It intensifies my D Vitamin
to good health.
Sun is fun – too many snippets
on skin – avoid.

RICHARD WRIGHT

1908 – 1960
BORN NEAR ROXIE, MISSISSIPPI

Growing up in a small Mississippi town, where
poverty persistently abounded...
never having enough to eat...
was a contentious battle for Richard to defeat.

Desperate for a better life,
his family moved many times, many places.
Arkansas, Jackson, Mi., Chicago, Memphis, Tennessee
Just to name a few.
Being black in the South... dictated a hard way of life.

Despite obstacles of discrimination, desperation,
dedredation, pain, shame and family battles,
a granny that worked over his child mind, Richard
procured an inspired desire to find himself.

He persevered through turbulance.
It was a heavy burden.
He was a quiet searching soul.
He possessed a yearning to read.
With a borrowed library card, he was ready to proceed.

Moving to Chicago did not dictate a better life.
Instead, he endured even greater strife.
One thing for sure...

when you're chocolate...
there's never enough milk...
to change the skin color.

Richard fostered an impulse to dream,
no one around him had ever seen.
Some thought he was crazy,
but his mind was never lazy.

His greatest desire was to become a writer.
He displayed enormous ability.
He studied great writers... he learned people.
All these elements provoked in Richard
a hunger to excel.
Richard had a burning yearning to express himself
on paper.

He was broken and beaten down many times.
No one could steal his thoughts, experiences
or his mind.

Despite hardships of pain, hunger, harsh treatments,
meaningless jobs, substandard housing and many
other maladies...

HE DREAMED ON!!!!

Next time you have a dream...
just wade through the nay-sayers, doubters, and
jealous minds of time.

Snatch a page or two from the books of
Richard Wright. Better yet, read some of his works
of genius.

Mr. Wright's most famous book "<u>Native Son</u>,"
published in 1940, sold 200.000 copies in less than
three weeks. In 1945 "<u>Black Boy</u>," was published
and was even more popular than "<u>Native Son</u>."

Richard Wright is considered one of America's best
writers of all times.

<u>DREAMS REALLY CAN BECOME REALITIES. SO, DREAM ON.</u>

IT'S NOT WHERE YOU ARE FROM.
IT'S NOT HOW FAST YOU RUN.
IT'S HOW FAR YOU COME.

DEALING WITH LIVING

The quality of best...
Flowed through me a chill.
At evening rest...
I did my best.
A thousand twilights
Have flashed, flickered and fluttered.
Hallowed melodies whisper...
Like the shaded winds-
Though daunting.
Energy cast itself a spell-
That dissipate down my spine,
Ever so gently.
The silence of splendor-
Twinkle to a savor delight.

One day my energy will relent
And release itself to a greater cause.
When no Parrot mimics... no more,
When the rapid springs
Reverberate ageless,
When the sun has given its best-
When the wind has gone to rest-
When my ultimate has
Reached its end... only after
I have exhibited my best.

"LOVE THAT WENT THE DISTANCE"

Jesus' love went all the way.
You can depend on it day after day.

Not just for a season...
But love being the reason.

He took his love all the way to Calvary's Cross.
Jesus paid the ultimate cost.

Diamonds and gold in the earth
Are no comparison to His Magnificent Birth.

Some of our love stops giving and doing at 50%
We allow ourselves to feel content.

His love takes you all the way.
His love is here to stay.

Love is not just a four-letter word.
It is the sweetest sound in nature, I have ever heard.

Sometimes love never speaks.
But could be the loudest sound you will frequently hear.

Love has many heads.
Love is loaded with legs.

Love has countless hands.
Love is willing to try again and again.

Love sometimes have tears.
Love may have fears.

Love is the strongest energy in the universe.

Love is seeing what is not there.
Love is embracing what's there.
Love is picking up what's left.

Love sees beyond the circumstances.
Love keeps searching for the invisible.

Love is never a stranger...
In a strange land.

Love is an unborn baby.
Trying to defy the abortionist's hands.

Love is talking without the lips always moving.
Love is apologizing without any offense.

Love is genuine, without getting in the way of sex.

Love is a divine creation...
Given freely by the creator.

When love is motivated, it moves.
Love is really very good news.

Love likes to connect.
Love doesn't always easily reject.

Love is not a current in the stream.
Love is the complete stream of life.

Love is not empty words.
Love is truth eager to be seen and heard.

Love is motivational.
Love is inspirational.

Love is trying to stop the pain.
Love is less concerned about self-gain.

Love is focused energy.
Love is a pointed and captivated way.

Love is not racial.
Love is not resentful of a false negotiator.

Love will release itself into every heart
That is willing to receive it.

Love is willingness of choice.
Love is a loud voice.

Love sees the ugly.
Love attempts to bring the beauty.

Love is planning for the good,
When the bad reigns supreme.

Love never stops giving.
Love began... should never end.

Love is building a boat.
Without having any water.

It is sometimes hard for love to deny.
It is often difficult for love to ask why.

Love is going the distance,
Without counting the milage.

Love is conclusive... no need to imagine.
Love is simply sharing and caring.

Love is a smile that radiates from the inside out.
Love should never be about self-doubt.

Love is a debt Jesus paid.
Love is a debt we owe.

Love is the willingness to believe.
Love is the eagerness to receive.

Love is heart focus.
Love is not a mind token.

Love is not ashamed... to be called by name.

<u>LOVE DISPELS HATE</u>

Love is not about beating yourself up
About giving it away.
Love is about transforming itself day by day.

Love is not about money well spent.
Love is defying the hints.

Love is not about the circle.
Love is the circle.

Love is not the hinge that swings the door.
Love is the hinge, the door, the house and
The creator of them all.

AS BOBBY AND SHERRY BURNETTE, MISSIONARIES
IN HAITI ALWAYS SAY, **<u>"LOVE IS SOMETHING YOU DO.</u>"**

"HAVE A LOVE DAY"

JESUS THE GREATEST LISTENER

Jesus the greatest listener stands bold.
His hearing never grows old.
He hears the smallest feather fall.
He hears the simple bird call.
He hears the whistle of the breeze.
Searing through the Mulberry trees.
He hears our every heartbeat.
This is such a nice treat.
Every negative word uttered... he heard.
So don't say anything you don't want God to hear.
Don't say things you might fear.
For, He holds every word dear.
Even when the cookie crumbles –
To Him it may sound like the loudest thunder.
He hears every tear that falls.
He is there for our smallest call.
So, hearing is a choice.
He gave each of us a voice.
Sickness listens to God.
when He says go it leaves.
Death listens to God.
When Jesus told Lazarus to come forth –
Death heard and left.
Blindness listens to God.
When Jesus cast out blind demons, they left.
Deafness relented its stand at Jesus' rebuke.
Lameness left at the voice of Jesus.
Sin relented and went when we repented.

God's ears never sleep
His hearing is very deep.
His ears are never too busy to hear.
His ears never grow weary of hearing.
His ears never need a check-up.
He doesn't wear hearing devices.
He is never confused by what he hears.
He is never shocked or surprised by what he hears.
He never had ringing in the ears...
Like I have today.

UGLY (VS) BEAUTY

Ugly is automatic,
but your beauty needs some working on.

When sin came in,
beauty relented (somewhat)...
ugly became dominate.

Beauty will always take precedence
over ugly.
Beauty is from God.
Ugly is from the devil.
Ugly is evil.
Beauty is Godly.

Beauty is the beginning.
After God created the sea and sea
creatures **(Genesis 1:21)** God saw that it was good.
God made the beast of the earth and creeping
things and God saw that it was good **(Genesis 1:25)**.
"And God saw every thing that he made, and behold,
it was very good and the evening and morning
were the six day," **(Genesis 1:31)**.

The 'Garden of Eden' a thing of beauty...
satan entered the garden and ugly came in.

Beauty remains supreme.
Ugliness is from the devil.

Ugly heeds ugly
Beauty blossoms beauty.

Ugly said "I can make these beautiful flowers die."
Beauty said "each year I will return them with even
more beauty."

Ugly killed Job's ten children.
Beauty restored his ten children.
Ugly said, "I will strike Job's body with boils."
Beauty said, "I will bring Job out and make his
skin like new again." God did.
(Read the book of Job).

Ugly (satan) caused Jonah to be swallowed by a big fish
(Jonah 1:17)
Beauty (the Lord) caused the fish to vomit Jonah upon
dry land. **(Jonah 2:10).**

Ugly tries to control.
Beauty is to behold.

Beauty is energy that carries good news.
Ugly is a sore bruise.
Beauty is a kind word.
Ugly can't wait to be heard.
Beauty is when God cleanses and make new.
Ugly is transparent through and through.
Beauty is real gold.
Ugly is foals gold.
Beauty wakes you up to a new day.
Ugly tries to take it away.

Beauty is a song to sing.
Ugly is a viper sting.

Beauty spreads itself wide.
Ugly simply makes one tired.

Beauty has a voluptuous smile
Ugly is naughtiness to a child.

Beauty is advantageous.
Ugly is outrageous.
Beauty will fight to stay.
Ugly wants to take away.
Beauty is wisdom.
Ugly is stupidity.
Beauty is health and wealth.
Ugly is sludge and grudge.
Beauty is a sweet dream.
Ugly is a horror scene.
Beauty dresses itself in ***Godly Attributes***
Ugly walks in and makes a sinful debut.
Beauty ministers.
Ugly is sinister.
Ugly creates strife.
Beauty steps in with a ***Godly Fight***.
Beauty is always a winner
Ugly is always a looser.
Beauty is love.
Ugly is hate.
Beauty is complimentary words.
Ugly just wants to be heard.
Ugly tries to steal the seed.

Beauty is the harvest from the seed.
Beauty is here to stay.
Ugly will die away.
Beauty comes from the center of **_Heaven_**.
Ugly comes from the pits of **_hell_**.

"I AM"

When the devil tries to take you out...
tell him what you are all about.

I am about God's love
I am about Joy
I am about Peace
I am about Happiness
I am about Faith
I am about Prayer
I am about Perseverance
I am about Overcoming
I am about Gratitude
I am about Prosperity
I am about Forgiveness
I am about Winning
I am about Power
I am about God's Business
I am about Control
I am about A Sound Mind
I am about His Mercy
I am about Healing
I am about Perfect Health
I am about Authority
I am about Fasting
I am about Respect
I am about The Great Life
I am about Everlasting Life
I am about Service

I am about Serving
I am about Repentance
I am about Confessing My Sins
I am about Increase
I am about Giving
I am about Wisdom
I am about Understanding
I am about Listening
I am about Learning

Actually... I have already won.
I know it.
The devil knows it.
God knows it.
I am about my Assignment.

**"He who has the son has life;
whoever does not have the Son
of God does not have life. I write
these things to you who believe
in the name of the Son of God,
so that you may know that you
have eternal life..."**

1 John 5:12-13

HIS UNFAILING FORGIVENESS

I know today and all days will be good,
because God planned, they would.
God did not create bad days.
Circumstances may dictate or shape your day.
Just have faith to believe,
when you do... you will receive.
There are no flaws in God's faith.
Faith works every time
and will give you peace of mind.
When I experience a dark place...
I know it's one I can face.
Because I know God is there.
I never need to ask where.
When you know what God is about...
you will never need to doubt.
Jesus already conquered all our fears.
Just jump up and give Him cheers.
When I didn't have a dime...
He came right on time.
When lacking food and shoes...
He knocked on my door with good news.
When I couldn't pay the rent...
He took care of that also.
When in pain... the Holy Spirit came.
His presence is like the rainbow...
after the storm... after the rain.

**"And forgive us our debts, as we forgive
Our debtors," (Matthew 6:12).**

LETTERS!!!

There are 26 letters out there––
floating around areas... looking
to be apprehended by words.

Letters for <u>Joy</u>,
Letters for <u>Peace</u>,
Letters for <u>Praise</u>,
Letters for <u>Prosperity</u>,
Letters for <u>Forgiveness</u>,
Letters or <u>Love</u>,
Letters for <u>Life</u>,
Letters waiting to become words.
Letters waiting to be owned by words.
Words to be released like rockets...
letters allocating themselves into greater dimensions...
to gather around... to talk about their own freedom.
No more sense of sorrow... instead, lending themselves
to sweetness.
Words emitting themselves to bulging adventures.
Simple objects can discharge words of energy...
and go into lovely poetry... a thing-au-ma-gig.
Waves of words tease the waters released by the sea,
to tell a story.
Poems are like the growing of limbs in movement.
The heating sunshine, glorifying a glass window.
They trample like grass underneath our feet...
waiting for functionality.

A pen to array exquisite words...
to ragger the inventiveness.
Only the poet will know, assuredly.
Letters will decide whether words flourish.
Letters will become astounding... as they
catapult themselves into words.

STOPS... ON YOUR WAY TO GREATNESS

STOP... listen to the trees...
    as they grow out their leaves.
STOP... to hear the calls from the wild...
    the cry of a little child.
STOP... to see the darkness of night fade dim...
    as a new day dawns.
STOP... as you pass grama's house...
    as she reclines on her couch.
STOP... listen to the raindrops drop, drop...
    and hear their plop, plop.
STOP... to understand where you are...
    before you step in front of a moving car.
STOP... to give a little smile...
    to a face that shows guile...
STOP... to offer a handshake of love...
    that comes from above,
STOP... to observe...
    what God has preserved.
STOP... to share a prayer...
    to show someone you care.
STOP... to give somebody a helping hand...
    it just may relieve their pain.
STOP... to achieve.
STOP... to receive.
STOP... where you stand...
    you can always start again.

STOP... to hear the Robin sing.

STOP... to pluck a flower in Spring.

STOP... before you decide to go.

STOP... observe the colors of the rainbow.

STOP... to listen to the lawn mow.

STOP... to encourage someone on their way...
     you don't have to stay.

STOP... on your way to greatness...
     you just may have achieved
     your goal at your *first stop*.

LIFE IS HEAVY!!!

Life is heavy!
So, Lighten up!
Infuse a little humor
into the heaviness
and smile.
"Laughter maketh merry like a medicine," according
to the Bible. (Read the book of Proverbs).
So, "Lets laugh and heal."
"Laugh a little... or laugh a lot."
(Proverbs 17:22) "A merry heart doeth good like
a medicine: but a broken spirit drieth the bones."

Eyes of humor makes
for a sunshiny day.
Feet of humor...
leads to a happy place.
Hands of joy, as poets often say,
"Tickle my fancy."
Lips of smiles...
brighten my day.
The heart fosters peace when imbued with love.
Love on the **inside** should **permeate** to the **outside**
and **show** itself with **good deeds**.
Let's soak up our time with **humor, smiles, laughter** and **love**...
as often as possible.

TEARS OF TIME

A thousand tears may cry and leave.
To the hem of God's garment. I constantly cleave.
When each time I make one bad decision...
in His constant care He gives provision.
God touches the mind to reason again...
so that each new day we can began again.

Deep down in the valley of low...
God can reach his touch and say, "let's go."
No need to stay and reason.
He is ready to bring you into a new season,
a time of complete bliss...
one you do not need to miss.

Over the years of time...
you can reverence a renewed mind,
of how God stopped the pain...
and filled your days with much gain.
Whenever the stain of disdain appears...
always remember, God is ever so near.

ME AND MY MIRROR

"Mirror, I did not consult you today.
I just hate seeing ex-rated, that way.
When I was young, we had some good fun.
Now you just stare back at me and remind.
You tell me that you did not change.
I just need to accept what remains."

"Twenty years ago, you gave me the impression...
I was just one hot number.
When I look at you now, I can only wonder.
When did the cookie crumble?
Was the beauty I thought I saw' just an illusion?
Did I draw the wrong conclusion?"

"Now you show me lines of change.
Dimples are now wrinkles...
sagging that don't mind lagging and
a belly that's now jelly."

"Mirror, I dare not look at you again.
We were once such good friends.
I could stare into you and stay.
Now, when I look at you... I know what you are
going to say." "Don't look at me that way...
let's just try and get along... come-what-may."

"Mirror, I could be cruel and break you,
but if one day I do...
embark on this journey and pursue, just remember...
I don't believe that stuff about... break a mirror...
seven years of bad luck.
"Um, I can't remember where I put my *Lucky Rabbit
Foot.*" (Smile).

"DON'T TRY TO FIGURE GOD OUT"

"JUST TRY TO FAITH GOD OUT."

God never said, "Have figures." Instead... God said, "Have faith,"
God is not a man. **(Numbers 23:19).**
We are not God.

People are finite:
Which means, we have <u>definable limits</u>.
God is infinite:
Which means, He is <u>subject to no limitations</u>. <u>Endless</u>.

God wants us to have the mind of Christ.
God did not give us everything.
If He did, we would know as much as He knows.
There would be no need for faith.

Our limited mind... is just that.
Man has figured out much... not apart from God.
Our knowledge capacity cannot hold everything God knows.

There's no need to try and figure God out.
Our need is to try and hold God out in our faith
until God says, "YES OR NO," OR, "IT'S TIME TO GO."

Sometimes our figuring may diminish our faith.
We don't want our figuring to get in the way of our faith.
We must seek God for energy and faith to hold out until
the end. Only then do we have the possibility to win.

DISCOURAGEMENT

It will come.
It visits with the wise.
It often frequents the sick.
It does not discriminate.
It troubles the rich.
It seems a constant companion to the poor.
It is color blind.
It can pop up like an unexpected shower of rain
It can creep upon the mind like a wild cat watching
it's prey.
It blazes the imagination like the scorching sun.
It can paralyze the body with stress.
It can sap your energy and strength.

I CALL IT DISCOURAGEMENT!!!

There is a reason, but
it is only for a season.
It is temporary.

The season will pass.
Sometimes real fast...
Sometimes real slow...
Just remember... it will go.

You may say...
"I feel down and out today."

"Just give God your down
and He will surely bring you out."

God can take away the prefix 'dis.'
He can take away the suffix 'ment,
from discouragement and give us the
the **root word courage.**

Remember God's Commandment

"Have not I commanded thee?
Be strong and of a good courage;
be not afraid, neither be thou dismayed:
for the Lord thy God is with thee
whithersoever thou goest." **(Joshua 1:9).**

"Wait on the Lord: be of good courage,
and he shall strengthen thine heart: wait,
I say, on the Lord." **(Psalm 27:14).**

Courage Can Build Confidence.

"And now, little children, abide in him;
That when he shall appear, we may have
confidence, and not be ashamed before him
at his coming." **(1 John 2:28).**

"And this is the confidence that we have in
him, that, if we ask any thing according to his
will, he heareth us:" **(1 John 5:14).**

Courage Will Produce Hope and Trust.

"Trust in the Lord with all thine heart; and lean not unto thine own understanding." **(Proverbs 3:5).**

"Blessed is the man that trusteth in the Lord, and whose hope the Lord is." **(Jeremiah 17:7).**

When discontent appears, God can cause it to disappear and bring contentment. "But godliness with contentment is great gain." **(1 Timothy 6:6).**

"Let your conversation be without covetousness; *and be* content with such things as ye have: for he hath said, I will never leave thee, nor forsake thee." **(Hebrews 13:5).**

Friends may disappear of appear, in your season of discouragement and pain. They may care or not care. They may not know the right words to say... as in the case of Job's three friends who came to visit Job in his hour of grief but brought little comfort.

Job 2:11
"Now when Job's three friends heard of all this evil that was come upon him, they came every one from his own place, Eliphaz, the Temanite, and Bildad the Shuhite, and Zophar the Naamathite for they had made an appointment together to come to mourn with him and to comfort him."

But these three brought Job no comfort. After hearing Their complaints...
Job answered

"Then Job answered and said, "I have heard many such things: miserable comforters *are* ye all." **(Job 16:1-2).**

God Will Comfort Us In Our Hour Of Disappointment

Jesus said to his disciples, "And I will pray the father, and he shall give you another comforter, that may abide with you for ever;" **(John 14:16).**

"I will not leave you comfortless: for I will come to you." **(John 14:18).**

"Casting all your cares upon him; for he careth for you." **(1 Peter 5:7).**

When God Brings Us Out Of Our Disappointment And Sadness We Can Tell Others About His Goodness.

"And the Lord said, Simon, Simon, behold Satan hath desired *to have* you, that he may sift *you* as wheat: But I have prayed for three, that thy faith fails not: and when thou are converted, strengthen thy brethren." **(Luke 22:31-32)**

God Wants Us To Rejoice And Give Him Praise

"Sing, O heavens; and be joyful, O earth; and break forth into singing, O mountains: for the Lord hath comforted his people, and will have mercy upon his afflicted. **(Isaiah 49:13)**

THAT CAT WAS A REAL GENTLEMAN

Under a blanketed night sky...
they ramble...right by...passer byes,
unknown... unnoticed... they stroll...
unsightly, to behold.

Carelessly knocking over trash cans,
exhibiting lack of remorse or pain...
sometimes receiving great gain,
whatever the bounty, they never complain.

They go traveling on to the next can...
without any feelings of disdain.
Some are strays all alone...
others are pets with homes.

This home asserted boastfully of 4 cats.
First cat sibling... *Mickey,* black and white, fat and old.
Next sibling cat... setting high on fridge, *Willie* the *Nellie.*
Perching luxuriously on precarious spots... sat *Davey.*

Willie and Davey streaked grey and black...
they were like identical twins, on sight.
They were sweet and neat.
You automatically knew they were kin.
They were as sweet as the wind.

Leo, color coated orange and white, rounded
out the fourth member of the clan. Leo... the lover.
What a gaily beautiful sight.
I never thought much about cats.
He probably thought he met his match.

I was caring for a family member.
Leo quickly learned by daily schedule.

Like clockwork each morning...
he would set in the window...
anticipating... awaiting my arrival.
His cat instincts were like golden morsels of wisdom.

Once my entrance was completed...
Leo would leap down and follow me.
After reaching my sitting place it was on.

After jumping on the table next to me ... his
cat whiskers would blaze my neck.
I knew what was next.
Wet cat nose touching my ear... neck...
such lingering sense of fanciful play.

This stuff... akin to great lovers.
Shakespeare's Romeo and Juliette,
Robert and Elizabeth Browning's
"How do I love thee? Let me count the ways,"
would need some working on.
He catted his way around by neck and ears.
A paw or 2 landed on my shoulders.

That cat was a real gentleman.
One would think he acquired his skills from
Cat University.
How else could he maneuver moves like that.

Some may say, "you shouldn't go there,"
but that feline never left a scratch.

Before anyone goes *critical or crazy*... think about that
hickey... the one you got from high school.
You *automatically* broke the rules.
That kiss you thought was bliss.
You thought him to be better than slice bread...
only to end up with a life of hell and dread.

Leo never instituted anything more.
After finishing his natural play...
he would exit the nearest door.
I never met a cat like that before.
I never met a cat like that since.
I never knew where he went.

Maybe he graduated to greater things.
Maybe he caught the attention of a female suitor.
Maybe he got fixed.
Perhaps, he never had cat children.
Perhaps, he made the big times.
Maybe he is dancing in the *antechambers* of cat history,
with a *cane* and *Stetson Hat*.
I shall never forget that cat.

"WE SHOULD NEVER FINISH OUR LIFE."

"WE SHOULD LET JESUS FINISH OUR LIFE."

God created the life of man...
with **Holy Love** in His hand.
Man was never meant to die.
But sin came in to defy.

When man began...
he was destined to win.
He possessed the attributes of the father.
He was complete without any bother.

God said, "the soul that sinneth, it shall die."
(Ezekiel 18:4).

A life of sin... should never have been.
Let God begin... your life again.

God gave his son. He was like the noon day sun.
The cross was no fun, but at the foot of the cross
life begun.

The father had purpose even before Jesus surfaced.
We have **purpose,** we have **potential**. We have **destiny**.

Why engage in careless activities that could be life
finishing?

Why sit on the side lines and watch the game of life
run by. Jump in and win.

The **Holy Spirit** will lead and guide us if
we so desire.

If you have never tried to
accomplish something... how do you know
you cannot?

So let Jesus pick up your life and begin again.

"MAN'S GREATEST GIFT"

The day of Jesus birth...
is the greatest gift to planet earth.
He departed his life from above,
with a grand journey steeped in love.

On **Planet Earth** people were deep in sin.
No one had a clue for a solution within.
In merry and pleasure, they believed.
They were completely unaware of what they
could receive.

Jesus walked, taught, gave and saved.
The **Angelic Host** were beaming with praise.
Jesus not only showed us the way.
He keeps doing it day after day.
Jesus is the key to **everlasting life.**

Some accept His gift of love.
Others reject His sacrifice, nevertheless,
He is our salvation from above.
His is the sweetest voice, I have ever heard.

For my every season... Jesus is the real reason.
With His precious life... He paid the ultimate price.

Whatever our needs... He is ready to heed.
We must simply **invite Him** in, when we do, we win.

So, why gamble on earth's sinking sand?
Use your faith for **Heavenly things;** they are grand.
Heaven is without limitations.
Read the book of **<u>Revelations</u>.**

(Revelations 21:19-27, 22:1-5).

Jesus is not just for a season.
<Jesus is the real reason.>

A BLACK WOMAN

Her speech is so kind.
This captivates the essence of her mind.
She possesses no shame.
She is most assuredly destined for fame.

The circumference of her lips encompasses her heart.
Circles of her smile radiates around the moon.
The curving of her jawbone...
the implanting of her teeth...
are like steel to build.

Those eyes sparkle like noonday sunshine
on rippling sea waves.
That spiced hair folds beneath the nape of
her strong neck.

Energy radiating through her being
equates a thousand lightning bolts.
It was birthed in her a divine strength.
Her stamina must carry her
through troubles untold and unseen.

The planting of her feet extends deep into Ebony Earth.
The progression of her steps dictates a long journey.
The urgency of her hands... outstretched.

The bend of her arm, to behold future generations.
Words from her mouth... roars like clasps of thunder.

Songs escaping her vocals implies sweet hope.
She rises from her encapsulated cocoon –
as Butterfly Wings mounts on Eagle Flights.

All that claim to know her may not.
All that don't know her may learn of her.
She knows that loosing is not her persona.
Winning is her gut instinct.
For all the times she loved and lost, she never once
gave up on the pursuit of hanging tough.

WHO AM I?

WHO ARE YOU?
WHAT DID GOD SAY?
WHOSE REPORT WILL WE BELIEVE?

God said... "We are beloved" **(1 John 3:1)**.

God said... "We shall be called the sons of God" **(1 John 3:1)**

God said... "Man is made in His image" **(Genesis 1:26-27)**.

God said... "We are the people of his pasture and the sheep of his hand" **(Psalm 95:7)**.

God said... "We are chosen vessels" **(Acts 9:15)**.

God said... "He hath made man a little lower than the angels and hath crowned him with glory and honor" **(Psalm 8:5, 6)**.

God said... "We are blessed" **(James 1:12)**.

God said... "He sanctified us" **(Jeremiah 1:5)**.

God said... "He made some of us apostles, and some prophets: and some evangelist: and some pastors and teachers" **(Ephesians 4:11)**.

God said... "We are sanctified, justified, washed" **(1 Corinthians 6:11)**.

God said... "We are a holy People" **(Deuteronomy 7:6)**.

God said... "If we do his will, we are His sister, brother, mother" **(Matthew 12:50)**.

God said... "We are a chosen generation, a royal priesthood a peculiar people for those he called out of darkness **(1 Peter 2:9)**.

Jesus said... "We are made kings and priest **(Revelations 1:6)**.

God said... "Jesus purchased us with His own blood, the Holy Spirit hath made us overseers to feed the church of God" **(Acts 20:28).**

God said... "Behold, now we are the sons of God, and it doth not yet appear what we shall be: but we know that, when he shall appear, we shall be like him: for we shall see him as he is." **(1 John 3:2).**

God said... "Go thy way: for he is a chosen vessel unto me to bear my name before the Gentiles, and kings and the children of Israel." **(Acts 9:15)**

God said... "And the Lord God said. It is not good that the man should be alone; I will make him an help meet for him. **(Genesis 2:8)**

God said... "For we are his workmanship," **(Ephesians 2:10).**

SO, NOW WE KNOW WHO WE ARE!!!!!!!

1. Made in the image of God
2. The sheep of his hand
3. The people of his pasture.
4. Chosen vessels.
5. Brothers, sisters and mother (of Jesus).
6. Made a little lower than the angels.
7. We are **blessed**.
8. We are **sanctified**.
9. We are **Justified**.
10. We are **Glorified**.
11. We are **cleansed**.
12. We are **holy**.
13. We are **chosen**.
14. We are **prophets**.
15. We are **preachers.**
16. We are **Evangelists.**
17. We are **teachers**.
18. We are **pastors.**
19. We are God's highest creation on earth.
20. **WE ARE ALL <u>ONE RACE,</u> (<u>THE HUMAN RACE</u>).**
21. We are a chosen generation.
22. We are a royal priesthood.
23. We are peculiar people.
24. We are daughters, sons, kings.
25. We are overseers.
26. We are **beloved**.
27. We are the children of God.
28. We are his workmanship.
29. Man (Adam) received a rib from God.
30. We are **Spirit, Soul** and **body**.

DOWN HERE ON PLANET EARTH

Down here on Planet Earth...
the origin of my flesh birth.
The spirit said to the flesh, "I'm coming down to
give it my best."

My body arrived on Earth Thanksgiving Day.
Perhaps my mother never planned it that way.
My spirit left its' Heaven Home and entered
my flesh dome.

My flesh contained everything bad.
The indwelling spirit tried to make it glad.
Of course, flesh and blood demanded to reign.
This made the spirit grieve with pain.

Many times, body and spirit clashed.
The crumbling flesh often crashed.
The flesh said, "spirit, I'm having my way."
The spirit said, "you will pay, maybe soon, maybe later,
but someday."

The spirit came to lead and guide.
The stubborn flesh is reeked with pride.
We must lay flesh aside,
because we know, flesh is not wise.

God, our creator, knows what's best.
Don't be led by flesh... it can only guess.
Before making a choice... it's always wise, to listen to His voice.

THE CHURCH: WHEN THE CHURCH ATTENDS THE HOUSE OF WORSHIP.

Ephesians 4:11, 12
"And he gave some apostles; and some prophets; and some evangelists; and some pastors and teachers;
For the perfecting of the saints, for the work of the ministry, for the edifying of the body of Christ."

The church spreads the Gospel.
The church prophesies.
The church evangelizes the world.
The church pastors in the house of worship.
The church teaches.
The church gets sick.
The church receives miracles of healing in the house of worship.
The church gives gifts of healing (Paul, Peter).
Some of the church have divers' sorts of tongues.
The church works on secular jobs.

The church are doctors.
The church are nurses.
The church has sex
The church has children.
The church goes to college.
The church talks, walks.
The church thinks,
The church gets angry.
The church travels.
The church eats, sleeps, buys homes, buys cars.

The church prays
The church sins, repents,
The church writes books.
The church cries, laughs.
The church experience happiness,
sadness, gets sick, must sleep,
exercise and eat.
The church sings, shouts and gets excited.

Romans 16:5

"Likewise greet the church that is in their house. Salute my well beloved Epaenetus, who is the first fruits of Achaia unto Christ.

The church meets in people's homes.
The church meets outside in open spaces.
The church can meet at any given time, anywhere.
The church can be one person or many people.

Acts 20:28

"Take heed therefore unto yourselves, and to all the flock, over the which the Holy Spirit hath made you overseers, to feed the church of God, which he hath purchased with his sown blood.

The church requires spiritual food.
Jesus purchased (us), the church, with his blood.
The church are we, they, him, her, us, and you.
The church goes to prisons and jails to minister.
The church is tall, short, fat and slim.
The church goes on diets to lose or gain weight.

Mark 13:26, 27

"And then shall they see the Son of man coming in the clouds with great power and glory."

"And then shall he send his angels, and shall gather together his elect from the four winds, from the uttermost part of the earth to the uttermost part of heaven."

**Jesus' bride (the church), shall be
caught up out of the earth to be with
the Lord.**

THE HOUSES OF WORSHIP

The houses of worship shall still stand, but the
church (the saints) will be with Jesus.
Man made buildings of worship.
They are made of wood.
They are made of stones.
Some are made of brick and mortar.
Others are made of all kinds of material.
Some are small.
They are large.
They are grand.
Some are just falling down shacks.
Many are beautiful with great architectural features.
They serve various functions.
They have different names.
People get married in them.
They are used for anniversaries.
They worship in them.
Some set on hills, others on flat land.
These structures will remain earth bound.

SOME OF MY VIEWS ON CERTAIN THINGS

If you **focus** long and hard enough on **trying** to **find something bad** in a person, **you will usually find it.**

If you focus long and hard on finding something good about a person, you will probably find it.

Is it **expedient to look** for and severely **analyze** every **flaw** in your **mate?** Let happiness and love permeate and flow.

You will never find everything in a mate that you think should be there... if you did, you would have found a perfect person, or an imperfect person.

Seek diligently and listen carefully for the voice of God.

God told the prophet Hosea to marry a whore. Hosea obeyed God and married Gomer (a prostitute). If God spoke to you, man or woman of God and told you to marry a pimp or a prostitute, what do you think you would do?

Love and marriage don't always come neatly wrapped in pretty packages.

Have you ever really asked God why you are single?
Have you ever really asked God why you are married?

You may have misconceptions about your mate; before making a final judgement, speak to them.

Is there a set time for a person to learn love? Some learn faster than others.

Some people's satisfaction is never satisfied.

- No matter how great it is... it's never great enough.
- No matter how wide it is... it's never wide enough.
- No matter how long it is... it's never long enough.
- No matter how high it is... it's never high enough.
- No matter how big it is... it's never big enough.
- No matter how pretty it is... it's never pretty enough.

At some point satisfaction may become necessary. It doesn't mean that's all there is or should be. It doesn't mean limitations. It just may mean satisfaction is necessary.

Can you give away something you don't have?
Can you give away something you do have?

If you think you really need to get to know that person before you say, **"I DO"** ... you really need to get to <u>know yourself first.</u> This could be the greatest gift you give to the both of you.

Impossible assumptions are just that... impossible, so, get over them, because someone else may already have. It's better never to assume anything.

The definition for happiness may not be the same for both of you, but both should know in advance.

Have you ever heard someone say, "the happiest day of my life was the day I got married?"

Have you ever heard someone say, "the happiest day of my life was the day I got divorced?"

Both the above statements could be true.

Aretha Franklin said "all she wanted was R-E-S-P-E-C-T when she got home." In marriage, each party should continually strive for mutual respect toward each other.

In the legal profession, there is a saying, *"if you act as your own attorney, you have a fool for a client."*

In dating and marriage, if you are only led by your own Intuition, it could be like lighting a dynamite fuse and waiting for the explosion.

<u>**Conversations are like cakes:**</u>
If you bake a cake and forget to put in the baking powder, it may not rise to the occasion.
In conversations, if he or she doesn't seem to be listening, you may have left out the main ingredient!!!

Everything doesn't always need to be taken to extreme to be good or great. <u>Expand your vocabulary</u>. <u>Learn another word</u>, it's called **moderation.**

If you bake a pie, you don't need to eat the whole pie in one setting, just one slice at a time. Life lived in moderation could be the key to survival.

Some people write books. They put a picture of themselves on the front and back covers of the book. They put the same photograph of themselves on every page in the book. "Did you become better looking from page *five* to page *fifteen*"? This could become a huge distraction from the message you need to convey.

"SO, WHAT'S THE POINT?"

- "Are you an old man beating the wind?"
- "Do you consider yourself a hottie?"
- "Is there some kind of disorder?"

"SO, WHAT'S THE POINT?"

Someone asked **John Wesley (founder of** the **Methodist Church)**, how he drew such large crowds when he preached. He stated **"I set myself on fire, and they come to see me burn."** "Now, that's hot."

Logic and wisdom can sometimes be intertwined. **The Temptations (a popular singing group)**, said, they could make a ship sail on dry land. **Noah (the Bible prophet),** was thought to be crazy, when he built a ship on dry land. "Where else would you build a ship, In the middle of the Red Sea?"

Noah's ship did sail, and 8 souls sailed on it, plus the animals. The Temptations imaginary ship never sailed. "I think they were just trying to impress the girls."

If sex sounds funny... leave off one **(n)** and the **(y)**, all you have left is **fun**.

It may sometimes seem all humanity is teetering on the brink of insanity. I think at times in life we may operate on the fringes of insanity. The problem is, trying to identify the fringes, but more so, know that they exist.

Sometimes a mate's expectations may not be too high, they just may be impossible.

Do you think your wife's female parts are not quite up to par?

- Her lips are not sumptuous enough.
- Her eyes are not dreamy enough.
- Her breasts are not large enough.
- Her walk is not sexy enough.
- Her voice is not romantic enough.

OR, do you think, God just didn't know what he was doing when He created her? **Is enough, ever enough?**

God put Adam to sleep and removed one of Adam's ribs and created woman. Could Adam's rib have had a defect? **(Genesis 2:21-23)**.

If God can live with his or her imperfections, why can't we?

If a man marries a woman 20 or 30 years younger than himself... she just may be the daughter he never had.

If a woman marries a man 20, 30 years younger than herself... he just may be the son she never had.

Below are quotes by some well known people and others not so well known as they weigh in on marriage. Some are hilarious... some are not, but they are, nevertheless, thought provoking.

"The ideal husband understands every word his wife doesn't say."
— Alfred Hitchcock

"Marriage is like trading the adoration of many for the sarcasm of one"
— Mae West

"Marry a man your own age; as your beauty fade, so will his eyesight."
— Phyllis Diller

"To catch a husband is an art; to hold one is a job."
— Simone de Beauvoir

"Husbands are like fires. They go out when unattended."
— Zsa Zsa Gabor

"I never married because there was no need. I have three pets at home which answer the purpose as a husband. I have a dog which growls every morning, a parrot which swears all afternoon and a cat that comes home late at night."
— Marie Corelli

"A successful man is one who makes more money than his wife can spend. A successful woman is one who can find such a man."
— Lana Turner

"Marriage is a fine institution, but I'm not ready for an institution."
— Mae West

"It doesn't matter what you do in the bedroom as long as you don't do it in the streets and frighten the horses."
— Mrs. Patrick Campbell (1865-1940)

"When you love someone, all your saved-up wishes come out."
— Elizabeth Bowen (1899-1973)

"By all means marry; if you get a good wife, you'll become happy, if you get a bad one, you'll become a philosophy."
— Socrates (died 399 BC)

"Keep your eyes open before marriage, keep them half shut afterwards."
— Benjamin Franklin (1706-1790)

"If there hadn't been women's we'd be squatting in a cave eating raw meat, because we made civilization in order to impress our girlfriends."
— Orson Wells (1915-1985)

"There is one thing more exasperating than a wife who can cook and won't and that is a wife who can't cook and will."
— Robert Frost (1874-1963)

"Let the wife make the husband glad to come home, and let him make her sorry to see him leave."
— Martin Luther (1483-1546)

NEVER SEVER THE UMBILICAL CORD

BETWEEN YOU AND GOD.

Umbilical Cord
Cord arising from the navel that
connects the fetus with the Placenta,
(Merriam Webster; Collegiate
Dictionary – Tenth Edition).

The umbilical Cord connecting God – (Hands on Creation), and man, created by God was never meant to be severed.

"God's Creation"
Genesis 1:3 And God said, "let there be light."
Genesis 1:6 And God said, "let there be a firmament in the midst of the water."
Genesis 1:11 And God said, "let the earth bring forth grass, the herb yielding seed, and the fruit tree yielding fruit after his kind."
Genesis 1:20 And God said, "let the waters bring forth abundantly the moving creature that hath life, and foul that may fly above the earth in the open firmament of heaven."
Genesis 1:24 And God said, "let the earth bring forth the living creature after his kind, cattle, and creeping things, and beast of the earth after his kind."
Genesis 2:7 And the Lord God formed man of the dust of the ground, and breathed into his nostrils the breath of life.
Genesis 2:18 And the Lord said, "it is not good that man should be alone; I will make him a help meet for him."

Genesis 1:27 "So God created man in his own image, in the image of God created he him; male and female created he them."

With all God's creation, God Spoke and things came into existence.
1. The running water
2. The earth
3. The swimming fish
4. The towering trees
5. The fruit trees
6. The birds
7. The cattle
8. The creeping things
9. Light
10. The flowering trees.

Only did God have direct contact, "**hands on**," with the creation of man.

God kneeled and scooped man from the soil of the earth – **hands on**.

With an exchange of breath from God to man – the cord of life was created between God and man. This was mouth to mouth resuscitation. This was The first **CPR. Man then became a living soul.**

MAN, AND GOD CONNECTION

Man lay dead and at **rest**,
before God gave him a **breath**.
With God's breath man's heart
started **pumping**.
With a breath his blood started **jumping**.
With a breath from God man's brain started
thinking.
With God's breath, his eyes started **blinking**.
With God's breath man's mouth started
talking.
With a breath from God, man's legs started
walking.
Man's stomach started **growling**.
Man's face started **smiling**.
Man's lungs filled with **air**.
He had oxygen to **spare**.
Man's liver started to **quiver**.
Man started to **jitter**.
Man's fingers started **moving**.
Man's feet started **grooving**.

**WHEN THE CORD BETWEEN GOD
AND MAN IS SEVERED, MAN BECOMES:**
Uncaring
His heart becomes void of love
His mind becomes lacking any sense of direction
His soul and spirit are wounded
His feelings have grown cold
He has no increase

His life goes blank
His entire being becomes a shaft, blowing in
every direction.
He is left with nothing.

COVID 19

It entered upon Planet Earth,
Unseen by the seeing eye,
Unheard by the hearing ear,
Tasteless by the tasting tongue,
Smell less by the scented nose,
Unsensed by the human brain,
Untouched by the human hand,
This deadly evil is known as the Corona Virus.

It possesses no gun yet shoots through the body.
There are no bullets, but it ravishes the organs.
There are no stones, yet it hits with deadly force.
It's not a knife with sharp blades, but it cuts through
The body with severe intensity.

Covid can rip through the body like hairbrush bristles
go through hair.

Instead of leaving, it keeps on cleaving.
It may run through communities like a quiet stream.
There is no doubt, it is mean.
It snatches one off guard with much vexation,
Clutching away at life.
It devastates. It is enfeebling. It humiliates.
Covid 19 does not discriminate.
It just moves around and retaliates.

The virus keeps on speaking.
We keep on seeking.
Experts make up medicine batches,
Seeking to get a needle to catch it.
All the while many sniffle and snuffle.

Corona virus has no shame.
We know this is no game.
God's human race frets.
The virus has no regrets.

Covid 19 has no passport, yet it travels national
and international.
It has no airplane ticket but latches on and rides free.

It frequents the best restaurants,
homes,
and kings' palaces,
with malice.
What on Earth can we do?
We cannot sue.

As the Bible states,
"The pestilence that walketh in darkness," (Psalm 91:6).
The noon-day bright.
The silence of night.

The uncertainty of our day,
can leave us in a bad way.
All who have battle and lost,
have certainly paid the ultimate cost.

After such devastating horror,
many are faced with unimaginable sorrow.

God said, "If my people, which are called by my name, shall humble themselves, and pray, and seek my face, and turn from their wicked ways, then will I hear from Heaven, and will forgive their sins, and will heal their land," (2 Chronicles 7:14).

FRINGES OF TIME

Living without *Pandemic*
would he the easy way out.
That faceless mass –
the freedom from an armless needle.
That easy air – breathing softly –
underneath a changing wind.

But Mr. and Mrs. *Pandemic* won't allow.
They keep bringing in their children,
daughter (**Delta**), son (**Omicron**).
We rush to tie their tubes –
to find birth control.
They strip out testicular to render sterilization.

We resume guessing, we test.
There's no time for rest.
We peer over the horizon –
for a spectacle of clean –
a washing away of this **Nightmarish Dream**.

The stock piling of medical artillery
awaits the spring budding.
Stains of lemonade anticipates
wedding up with champaign, **nevertheless**,
the stockpile will fray.

We chew on the hambones
of our language – English for me.
When it's all over,
<u>the fool will still meddle in his folly</u>.

"SNUFFED OUT OF HUMAN EXISTANCE FOR WANT OF NEED"

Circumstances can hardly perceive
the want of a need.
One can dress and express their mind
in the courts of the intervention of time.
A want can waver...
a need to savor.
One can be just as urgent as the other.
One can survive alongside another.
Sometimes they may be interchangeable.
One can overlap the other.
The want is prevalent... as the need persist...
such as the want to breathe...
becomes the need to breathe.
The need to breathe...
becomes the want to breathe.
Embedded in the souls of humankind...
a free breath of air.
A God given right, an innate entitlement.
A free breath of oxygen... a God given.
When restricted of air, the heart
struggles to beat... to do its' job.
A deprivation of oxygen to the brain,
lungs, other organs cry out for air.
A desperation pursued for the entitlement...
for the freedom of God's air.

who made man a god to announce
to my heart... my skin is the wrong color?
I must never breathe again.
The heart knows no color.

It simply has a need and want for air.
Who made you a human god to separate
me from my natural entitlement of oxygen?
The Bible states, "The devil comes to steal, kill and destroy."

He begged for his God given right to breath... **that day**.
Many heard his cries go unnoticed, unanswered.
The perpetrators snuffed out his human existence...
on a public street for all to see.
The perpetrators acted as judge, jury and executioner... **that day**.
They denied the victim his day in court.
The gavel never hit the judge's desk.
The court never convened.
The trial date never hit the docket.
The jury was denied the evidence.
The death sentence had already been carried out.
The body went lymph, unresponsive.

The crowds were obliterated.
The world watched in shock and horror.
"The **perpetrators had taken all the victim's air –**
as *they continued to breathe freely*." "*That Day*."

Printed in the United States
by Baker & Taylor Publisher Services